Original title:
The Lullaby Lagoon

Copyright © 2024 Creative Arts Management OÜ
All rights reserved.

Author: Adrian Caldwell
ISBN HARDBACK: 978-9916-90-398-8
ISBN PAPERBACK: 978-9916-90-399-5

Cradle of Serene Silence

In the stillness where shadows play,
Soft whispers weave through the grey.
Stars blink gently, a lullaby's call,
Embracing the night, gently they fall.

Moonlight dances on the calm sea,
Wrapped in dreams, wild and free.
Lulled by the breeze, the world holds its breath,
Finding peace in this quiet depth.

Hush of the Midnight Shore

Waves murmur secrets to the sand,
As night wraps its arms, gentle and grand.
Footprints erased by the tide's gentle sweep,
In whispers of darkness, the ocean does keep.

Stars reflect in the water's embrace,
Time slips away in this timeless space.
The moon hangs low, casting soft light,
In the hush of the midnight, all feels right.

Ocean's Heartbeat at Dusk

Beneath a canvas of fiery hues,
The ocean breathes, a tranquil muse.
Colors blend in the fading light,
Echoing rhythms through the night.

The horizon blushes, kissed by the sun,
Waves cradle dreams as day is done.
Listen closely, hear the sound,
Of the ocean's heartbeat, profound.

Out of Time at the Water's Edge

Where day meets dusk on the water's crest,
Time stands still, a moment blessed.
Feet in the sand, hearts intertwined,
Lost in wonder, forever enshrined.

Ripples ripple, secrets spill,
Whispers of love in the evening chill.
Each wave a promise, each breeze a sigh,
In this sacred space, we fly high.

Twilight Tranquility and Stars

As daylight fades, a hush descends,
Soft whispers dance on evening's breath,
A tapestry of dreams begins,
In twilight's peace, we find our rest.

The stars appear, like tiny sparks,
They dot the sky in silver hues,
Each twinkle tells a tale of old,
Of love and loss, and hopes renewed.

A gentle breeze through branches sways,
The moonlight bathes the world in calm,
Nature sings a lullaby sweet,
In this embrace, we find our balm.

Beneath the vast, eternal dome,
We sit and dream, our hearts at ease,
The universe, a fitting home,
In twilight's glow, our spirits tease.

Swirls of Calm in the Inky Blue

Beneath the sky, so deep and vast,
The waves of night begin to swell,
In swirls of calm, the moments cast,
A peaceful breath, a soothing spell.

The stars entwine in cosmic dance,
A ballet spun with threads of light,
Each sparkle holds a fleeting chance,
To dream anew, to take to flight.

Whispers of wind through pine trees hum,
As shadows play in twilight's glow,
The night invites, a gentle strum,
Where all the world's worries can go.

In inky blue, where silence reigns,
We find our way, we seek what's true,
With every breath, the peace remains,
In swirling calm, we start anew.

Reflections in the Silent Cove

In a cove where shadows play,
Whispers linger, soft and gray.
Mirrored waters, calm and deep,
Secrets held, the silence keeps.

Pebbles dance beneath the tide,
Nature's art, where dreams reside.
Glimmers weave through emerald leaves,
Time stands still, the heart believes.

Waves retreat, the echoes fade,
Footprints left, a path we laid.
Softly sighs the evening breeze,
In the cove, we find our ease.

Gazes meet beneath the sky,
In this haven, moments sigh.
Reflections stir, the soul awakes,
In silent cove, our heart partakes.

Breezes of the Soothing Shore

Upon the shore where soft winds flow,
Gentle whispers, secrets grow.
Sand in toes, the sun will warm,
Nature's hug, a perfect balm.

Seagulls dance on waves of light,
Every moment feels so right.
Clouds drift by, a cotton dream,
Together woven, like a seam.

Shells and treasures, spill the tide,
With every wave, the stories hide.
Breezes carry, laughter's tune,
Underneath the silver moon.

In this space, we find our way,
Breezes guide both night and day.
Life renewed, in every breath,
Soothing shore, we conquer death.

Dreams Drifted on the Current

Floating softly on the stream,
Every ripple, a whispered dream.
Leaves that dance in twilight's grace,
In this moment, we find our place.

Currents pull where hopes reside,
Gentle waves that will not hide.
Stars reflecting in cool waters,
Telling tales of ancient authors.

As shadows blend with the night,
Dreams take flight, a wondrous sight.
Drifting onward, hearts align,
In the current, we combine.

Every thought, a soft caress,
Floating free, no need to stress.
In this flow, we feel the spark,
Dreams drift on, igniting dark.

Nightfall's Gentle Embrace

As daylight fades, a hush descends,
Wrapped in twilight, time suspends.
Stars awaken, a silver sheen,
Nightfall's whispers, soft and keen.

Moonlight spills on tranquil land,
Every shadow, subtly planned.
Crickets sing their serenade,
In the dark, new paths are made.

Embrace the quiet, let it mend,
In stillness, hearts begin to blend.
Each breath taken, a calming sigh,
In the night, we learn to fly.

Together in this gentle space,
Nightfall's love, a warm embrace.
With every star, our dreams ignite,
In the dark, we find the light.

Echoes of a Soft Serenade

Whispers dance in twilight's glow,
Notes that drift, like softest snow.
Hearts entwined in dreams untold,
In melodies, our love unfolds.

Stars above in harmony,
Calm the night, set spirits free.
Gentle breeze weaves through the trees,
Carrying our sweet decrees.

Each echo sings of days gone by,
Of laughter shared, a soft goodbye.
In every chord, a memory lies,
A serenade that never dies.

So let the music play along,
In every heart, we find our song.
Together in this twilight haze,
We are echoes through endless days.

Cradle of Celestial Waves

Beneath the sky, where dreams arise,
The moon reflects in tranquil tides.
Each wave whispers to sandy shores,
A cradle where the heart explores.

Stars light paths on oceans dark,
Guiding souls with gentle spark.
In breezes soft, we find our way,
Upon this cradle, night and day.

Ebb and flow like breath divine,
In salt and foam, our hearts align.
With every whisper, nature sways,
We dance within these timeless waves.

The cosmos hums a lullaby,
While dreams unfurl and spirits fly.
In this embrace, we drift and sway,
Forever lost in celestial play.

Slumber Songs Beneath the Stars

Softly wrapped in night's embrace,
Cradled in a starlit space.
Whispers of the lullabies,
Cradle dreams that gently rise.

Moonbeams cast their silver light,
Guiding us through the tranquil night.
In the stillness, hearts unite,
With every breath, pure delight.

Rustling leaves, a gentle tune,
Swaying softly 'neath the moon.
As the world fades far away,
We drift on slumber's sweet ballet.

Time stands still in this serene,
Beneath the stars, we find our dream.
In this haven made of grace,
Our hearts sing in the night's embrace.

Melodies of a Drowsy Bay

In a bay where soft tides play,
Gentle rhythms greet the day.
As sunlight spills on tranquil seas,
Drowsy waves hum sweet melodies.

Seagulls call in the warm, soft air,
While breezes dance without a care.
In this place where time stands still,
Joy blooms bright, like daffodil.

Sails drift by, like dreams set loose,
Each whisper tells a tale astute.
In every lull between the sways,
Echoes rise of lazy days.

With every note, the heart finds peace,
In the bay, our souls release.
This melody, a soft ballet,
Forever in our hearts will stay.

Slumbering Currents of the Night

In whispers deep, the river sighs,
Stars above like watchful eyes.
Moonlit ripples softly play,
While shadows dance and drift away.

The night unfolds its velvet cloak,
As dreams arise and silence spoke.
A gentle breeze through branches weaves,
Cradling hopes like falling leaves.

Beneath the surface, secrets sleep,
Where ancient tales in silence keep.
The water churns, a timeless flow,
In slumber deep, the currents know.

Rest now, dear heart, the night is still,
Embrace the quiet, let time will.
Awaken dreams within the dark,
In slumbering currents, find your spark.

The Quiet Symphony of Still Waters

The lake reflects a mirror's grace,
Nature's calm in a gentle space.
Ripples hum a soft refrain,
In harmony, they kiss the plane.

Cattails sway in the evening light,
Wings of birds take peaceful flight.
Notes of silence fill the air,
A symphony beyond compare.

Beneath the surface, life abounds,
In every whisper, joy resounds.
Emerald hues in tranquil pools,
Stilled moments that nature rules.

Reflections of a world so bright,
In still waters, hearts take flight.
The quiet song, serene and clear,
In every breath, the world draws near.

Shadows of Serenity at Dusk

As daylight fades, the shadows grow,
A gentle hush, a dreamy glow.
The dusk, it weaves a soft embrace,
Upon the earth, a tranquil grace.

Orange skies meet evening blue,
A canvas where the stars break through.
Whispers linger in the breeze,
Pine and cedar sway with ease.

The crickets chirp their evening tune,
While fireflies flicker 'neath the moon.
In twilight's calm, the world takes pause,
Embracing night without a cause.

Breath in the peaceful dusk's retreat,
Where shadows dance and hearts can meet.
In serene moments, lost and found,
A quiet love in silence bound.

Tidal Tranquility's Embrace

Waves caress the sandy shore,
With every rise, a gentle roar.
The ocean breathes a rhythmic sigh,
In tides that ebb, in dreams that fly.

Moonlit nights bring calm to be,
Where peace drifts free, and spirits sea.
Each splash a note of nature's song,
Echoing where we all belong.

Soft whispers of the rolling sea,
Finding solace, wild and free.
The salt-kissed air begins to weave,
Tidal tales for hearts that believe.

In tranquil waters, dreams take flight,
In waves of calm, we find our light.
Embrace the tides, let worries cease,
In tidal tranquility, discover peace.

Shimmering Sands of Slumber

Golden grains beneath my feet,
Whispers of the night so sweet.
Stars above in velvet skies,
A dreamland calls, where silence lies.

Waves that kiss the shore with grace,
Moonlight dances, a soft embrace.
In the twilight, shadows blend,
A tranquil realm, where dreams ascend.

Seashells sing of stories past,
Echoes of the ocean's cast.
Breezes hum a lullaby,
Inviting slumber, soft and shy.

In this hush of nature's charm,
The heart finds peace, away from harm.
Rest your soul on sands so grand,
In the shimmering sands of slumber's land.

Melodies of the Midnight Waters

Gentle ripples, silver light,
Songs of water, pure delight.
Moonbeams play upon the lake,
Nature's chorus, softly wake.

Whispers weave through willow trees,
Carried softly by the breeze.
Every splash, a note in tune,
A symphony beneath the moon.

Stars reflect on liquid glass,
Time stands still as shadows pass.
In the stillness, secrets bloom,
Melodies dispel the gloom.

Echoes linger, hearts take flight,
In the embrace of tranquil night.
Midnight waters paint the grace,
Melodies in time and space.

Cradle of the Celestial Sea

In the depths where starlight glows,
Dreams take flight, the heart bestows.
Each wave cradles whispers sweet,
A celestial haven, calm and fleet.

Beyond horizons, vast and wide,
Wonders of the cosmos hide.
Galaxies in azure swirled,
A cradle of a glittering world.

Tides that pulse with cosmic grace,
Time and space in warm embrace.
Where thoughts drift like ships at ease,
In the cradle of the celestial seas.

Starlit waters gently sway,
Guiding lost souls along the way.
In the calm, all fears released,
Here in the cradle, hearts find peace.

Harmony of the Surging Tides

Rhythms clash in nature's song,
Surging tides, where souls belong.
A dance of foam and crashing roar,
Wild and fierce, yet to explore.

Beneath the surface, life abounds,
In currents deep, where magic sounds.
Echoes of the ocean's might,
Drawing dreams from day to night.

Riding waves like songs unfurled,
Harmony in nature's world.
Every swell whispers a tale,
Of distant lands and winds that sail.

In the ebb, in the flow we find,
The unison of heart and mind.
A symphony of liquid grace,
In the harmony of tides, we trace.

Nap Time Under the Celestial Canopy

Underneath the starry night,
The world slows down to dream.
Crickets sing a lullaby,
In the moon's gentle beam.

Clouds drift softly overhead,
Whispers of the night air.
Blankets of calmness spread,
In this tranquil lair.

The world holds its breath in peace,
As wishes dance and gleam.
Time slows down, moments cease,
Cradled in a dream.

With every star, a story told,
Each flicker holds a sigh.
In this haven, hearts unfold,
Beneath the endless sky.

Driftwood Dreams and Silvered Waves

On the shore where whispers play,
Driftwood tells of tides gone by.
Silver waves in soft ballet,
Beneath the vast, blue sky.

Footprints drawn in golden sand,
Stories of a fleeting day.
The ocean's gentle hand,
Calls the sunset's brilliant ray.

Seagulls wheel in quiet flight,
Embracing evening's glow.
Dreams take wing, sail into sight,
As day takes its final bow.

Each breath of wind brings new delight,
The horizon's art displayed.
In the dance of day and night,
Peacefully, we are swayed.

The Soft Embrace of the Evening Sea

Whispers rise from evening sea,
As shadows lengthen on the shore.
The sun bows down, a symphony,
While waves caress forevermore.

Softly the tide pulls away,
Leaving treasures, shells and grain.
In twilight's kiss, the colors play,
Nature's canvas, love's refrain.

Footsteps linger, hearts entwined,
Each heartbeat echoes the sound.
In this moment, time is blind,
As love and sea are profound.

The scent of salt, a soothing balm,
Embraces all who call it home.
In the twilight's peaceful calm,
Our spirits freely roam.

Gentle Rhythms of the Resting Sands

Sands whisper tales of days gone,
Underneath the sunlit sky.
Each grain a memory, drawn,
As the tide flows and sighs.

Dunes rise, soft hills of time,
Crafted by the ocean's play.
A melody, a gentle rhyme,
In the light of fading day.

Gentle breezes stroke the land,
Awakening dreams once cherished.
In the stillness, hand in hand,
Hopes and moments, never perished.

Let the sunset paint the hour,
With colors bold and stark.
In the sands, we find our power,
Etched beneath the dark.

Resting Place of the Dreaming Tide

Upon the shore where dreams abide,
Soft whispers blend with the ocean tide.
The seagulls cry, a lullaby,
As stars awake in the velvet sky.

Waves caress the sands so warm,
In quietude, there's a gentle charm.
Each grain a story, each breath a sigh,
At the resting place where dreams will fly.

Enchanted Repose by the Sea

Beneath the boughs of swaying palms,
The ocean sings its soothing psalms.
Gentle breezes kiss the shore,
In this haven, we long for more.

Shells scatter tales from ages past,
While tides embrace, steadfast and vast.
Here in repose, hearts find their peace,
As time slips softly, never to cease.

Harmonies of the Whispering Current

In shadows cast by moon's embrace,
The water hums a tranquil grace.
Ripples dance in gleaming light,
A serenade through the starry night.

Whispers weave through reeds and sand,
A symphony of nature, grand.
With every wave, a tale unfolds,
In harmony, the current holds.

Naptime in the Moonlit Cove

In the cove where shadows play,
Moonlight drapes the night in gray.
Crickets sing their lullabies,
As slumber beckons 'neath the skies.

The waves rock gently, soothing, slow,
In this embrace, the world lets go.
Dreams take flight on silver beams,
Naptime whispers, cradle of dreams.

Whispers of Midnight Waters

In the dark, the waters sigh,
Gentle ripples, soft and shy.
Stars above, a glittered lace,
Embracing night in quiet grace.

The moon dips low, a silver thread,
Weaving tales of dreams unsaid.
Echoes dance on liquid glass,
As shadows blend with the night's mass.

The breeze carries secrets old,
Of tales that the night is told.
Beneath the surface, whispers flow,
In midnight's tale, we come to know.

Lost in thought, I drift away,
Where midnight waters softly play.
In every wave, a story swells,
The heart of night, where magic dwells.

Serenade of Silken Tides

A melody on ocean's breath,
Softly lingers, free from death.
The waves compose their gentle song,
In silken tides, they drift along.

Underneath the silver glow,
Tales of love and hope will flow.
Each tide a whisper on the shore,
A serenade forevermore.

Seagulls cry in rhythmic flight,
Joining the dance of day and night.
With each crest, the waters rise,
A symphony beneath the skies.

As day unfolds, the tides will change,
But in their song, we'll never range.
The ocean's pulse, a heart of dreams,
A serenade, where magic seems.

Dreams Adrift on Tranquil Shores

Upon the sand, where silence reigns,
Dreams drift softly, free from chains.
With every wave, a wish is cast,
On tranquil shores, where moments last.

The horizon glimmers, gold and blue,
A canvas vast, where hopes renew.
Footprints linger on the beach,
Life's fleeting breath within our reach.

Cradled by the ocean's song,
In our dreams, we all belong.
The tides will tell of journeys bold,
As stories weave, like threads of gold.

And in the hush of twilight's glow,
We'll find the peace the heart does know.
On tranquil shores, we breathe and sigh,
In dreams adrift, we learn to fly.

Moonlight's Gentle Caress

Beneath the moon's soft, tender light,
The world transforms into the night.
Shadows waltz on paths of blue,
A gentle caress, pure and true.

Whispers float on the evening breeze,
In every rustle of the trees.
The stars peek out, a twinkling dance,
Inviting hearts to take a chance.

Dreams awaken in silver beams,
Illuminating longing dreams.
With each heartbeat, time stands still,
Under the spell of moonlit thrill.

As night unfolds, the magic glows,
In moonlight's arms, our spirit flows.
A gentle caress, soft and sweet,
In the night's embrace, our souls meet.

Gentle Ripples of Reverie

Whispers dance upon the pond,
A soft embrace in twilight fond.
Dreams like shadows glide and sway,
In gentle ripples, night turns gray.

Stars above, a silver thread,
Ties our thoughts where silence bled.
In fleeting moments, peace we find,
As echoes linger, unconfined.

The water hums a lullaby,
To whispered hopes that drift and sigh.
In every glimmer, tales unfold,
Of hearts once brave, now softly rolled.

Let go your burdens, breathe in deep,
In tranquil waves, find joy to keep.
With every ripple, time stands still,
In reverie's embrace, we are filled.

A Dance of Starlit Waves

The ocean calls beneath the sky,
Waves that shimmer, dance, and fly.
Each crest a glint of silver light,
A symphony of dark and bright.

Moonlit whispers touch the shore,
Secrets shared forevermore.
With every crash and playful glide,
Nature's heartbeat, side by side.

In the coolness, shadows play,
Guided softly by the ray.
As tides embrace the sandy coast,
We lose ourselves, we learn to boast.

Amidst the stars that twinkle bold,
Stories of the night unfold.
We twirl with waves in sweet embrace,
In this dance, we find our place.

Calm Reflections in the Night

Beneath the stillness of the moon,
Lies a world, serene and strewn.
Mirrors frame the night's delight,
In calm reflections, thoughts take flight.

Ripples whisper secrets low,
In quiet pools where dreamers go.
The stars above, a patient guide,
In endless depths, our souls confide.

A lantern glows, a beacon fair,
Its soft light dances in the air.
In every flicker, we are shown,
How to wander, yet stay home.

In the beauty of this night,
We glimpse the echoes, pure and bright.
Within the calm, we find our way,
As shadows blend and softly sway.

Silhouettes of Slumbering Shores

Upon the edge where water meets,
Silhouettes rest in quiet beats.
With each wave, a soft embrace,
As dreams unfold in twilight space.

The tide, a soft and rhythmic hum,
Calls the weary to succumb.
Each grain of sand a timeworn tale,
Of love and loss, of ships that sail.

In shadows deep, the world stands still,
As night's enchantment starts to thrill.
Whispers of breezes intertwine,
In this moment, hearts align.

A canvas painted dark and bright,
Where dreams arise to take their flight.
Beneath the stars, we close our eyes,
On slumbering shores, where peace lies.

Secrets Beneath the Starlight

Whispers dance in the midnight glow,
Hidden tales from long ago.
Stars like gems in velvet skies,
Guard the dreams of silent sighs.

Shadows flicker, stories told,
Secrets wrapped in silver cold.
Beneath the light, we search and seek,
In the silence, hearts will speak.

Moonlight weaves a tapestry,
Of hopes and dreams and mystery.
Each twinkling star a friendly guide,
Leading souls where truths abide.

In the night, we find our place,
With every twinkle, soft embrace.
Secrets whispered on the breeze,
Starlit nights, our hearts at ease.

Shush of the Calm Waters

Starlit skies reflect the sea,
Peaceful waves, a gentle plea.
Ripples sing of tales untold,
In the night, brave hearts unfold.

The moon casts light on every crest,
As whispers cradle, lull to rest.
Softly rocking, dreams take flight,
In the embrace of tranquil night.

Around the shore, the shadows play,
Guiding ships that drift away.
Silent songs, a soothing balm,
In the stillness, hearts feel calm.

Quiet moments, a world in trance,
In water's shush, we find our chance.
To listen close to what we feel,
In calm waters, dreams reveal.

Nurtured by the Nautical Night

Underneath the twinkling stars,
The sea embraces, fights and spars.
Waves carry tales of pirates bold,
And dreams of treasures made of gold.

Nautical night, with its gentle sway,
Cradles secrets lost in the spray.
With sailing ships that cut through mist,
We touch the sky, and none resist.

Nurtured by the ocean's song,
We find a place where we belong.
Guided by the lighthouse beam,
In salty air, we dare to dream.

Stars overhead like guardians stand,
As the sea lends us a loving hand.
Nautical night, a warm embrace,
In its heart, we find our place.

Caress of the Ocean's Whisper

Whispers of the ocean's breath,
Carry tales of life and death.
Softly cradling every tale,
With each wave, the stories sail.

The sea caresses in the night,
Gentle kisses, pure delight.
A melody of salty air,
In her arms, we have no care.

Moonlit paths on water glide,
As dreamers find their hearts open wide.
Ocean's whisper, a siren's call,
Inviting us to rise, not fall.

In embrace of dusk's soft sheen,
We lose ourselves, where we have been.
With every wave, the world feels right,
In the caress of the ocean's night.

Tides of Comfort and Care

The waves whisper gently, a lover's sigh,
Rolling in soft, like the night sky.
Each ebb and flow brings a soothing balm,
Embracing the shores with a tender calm.

The moon casts its glow on the tranquil sea,
Guiding lost souls, like you and me.
In the dance of the tides, we find our place,
A refuge of warmth in this vast space.

With each crashing wave, worries dissolve,
In the waters of comfort, our hearts resolve.
The rhythm of nature, a healing art,
Bringing us closer, heart to heart.

So let us cherish this moment we share,
In the tides of love, in the winds of care.
Together we stand, come what may,
In the embrace of the sea, we'll forever stay.

Soft Shadows on the Silken Sand

The sun dips low, painting skies with gold,
Shadows stretch long, a story untold.
Footprints wander where the tide retreats,
Soft whispers linger where ocean meets.

Silken sand dances beneath our feet,
Each grain a memory, a moment sweet.
In the fading light, our laughter plays,
Echoing softly through twilight's haze.

The horizon glows with a lover's hue,
Carried by breezes, dreams come true.
We build castles, with hearts in hand,
In the magic of night upon the sand.

As darkness falls and the stars appear,
We hold close the warmth, love's tender cheer.
In soft shadows, under skies so grand,
Together we wander, hand in hand.

A Refuge in the Midnight Surf

Underneath the silver glow above,
The ocean's whispers tell tales of love.
Each wave a secret, a soothing song,
In the midnight surf, we find where we belong.

The cool breeze carries the scent of the sea,
Wrapping around us, wild and free.
In the moon's embrace, our worries fade,
In this refuge found, we are unafraid.

The rhythm of water lulls us near,
Every crash a promise, every splash a tear.
Together we dance in the ocean's light,
A symphony of stars, a breathtaking sight.

In the embrace of night, our spirits soar,
With the ocean's heartbeat, we crave for more.
In the depths of its waves, we feel alive,
A love reborn with each tide we dive.

Woven Dreams Across Ocean's Surface

Across the waves, our dreams take flight,
Woven in whispers, kissed by light.
The sea reflects our hopes so bright,
In the tapestry of stars, we find our sight.

Gentle currents carry wishes away,
To distant shores where wishes lay.
Each crest and trough tells a story new,
In the ocean's embrace, our hearts break through.

With each sunset that graces the sky,
We gather our dreams as the night draws nigh.
In the depths we wander, lost but found,
In the woven dreams, our love is crowned.

So let the tides guide us on our way,
Through night and day, come what may.
In the ocean's cradle, we will forever weave,
A tapestry of hope that we believe.

Swaying Palms in the Night

Beneath the stars, the palms do sway,
Whispers of night, they dance and play.
Moonlight glimmers on tranquil seas,
Carried gently on warm night breeze.

Shadows stretch across the sand,
Nature's beauty, so pure and grand.
A tranquil world, so calm, so bright,
In the embrace of the silver night.

Songbird Serenades by the Shore

Morning breaks with a soft, sweet tune,
Songbirds greet the dawning moon.
Fluttering wings in the golden light,
Melodies soar into the height.

On the shore, their voices blend,
Nature's songs, they never end.
Whispers soft of hope and cheer,
In the air, their dreams appear.

Lullabies from the Distant Wave

Waves crash softly on the shore,
Each one sings of tales of yore.
Gentle lullabies, they weave,
Softly coaxing dreams to leave.

Underneath a blanketed sky,
Restful breezes drift and sigh.
With each rise, with every fall,
The ocean's whispers cradle all.

Currents of Sweet Serenity

Flowing streams with a gentle grace,
Nature's calm finds its embrace.
In the quiet, peace will bloom,
As whispers chase away the gloom.

Underneath the swaying trees,
Breezes dance and weave with ease.
In this haven, hearts entwine,
Finding solace, so divine.

Voyage to Dreams Uncharted

In twilight's glow, we set our sail,
With whispered winds, we ride the pale.
Across the waves, our spirits soar,
To find the shores of dreams in store.

Stars alight in velvet skies,
Guiding us with twinkling eyes.
Each wave a tale, each gust a song,
In this vast void, we shall belong.

Through tempests fierce and calms so sweet,
With courage strong, our hearts will beat.
For every storm will pave the way,
To uncharted realms where dreams can play.

So raise the anchor, let us roam,
In dreams unknown, we find our home.
The voyage calls, our spirits gleam,
Together, we will chase the dream.

A Gentle Bath of Moonlight

The silver beams on waters dance,
A soft embrace, a tranquil chance.
In night's caress, the world reveals,
A gentle bath where silence heals.

Whispers weave through trees so tall,
As shadows stretch and nightbirds call.
Each glowing ray, a tender touch,
In moonlit nights, we feel so much.

The stars like jewels adorn the sky,
While dreams take flight, they softly sigh.
In this cocoon of quiet grace,
We find our peace, our sacred space.

Let worries fade like distant shores,
Within this glow, our spirit soars.
In moonlight's arms, we're always free,
A gentle bath, just you and me.

Constellations Over the Deep

Beneath the arch of endless night,
The constellations gleam so bright.
Each star a story, old yet new,
In cosmic tales, we wander through.

The ocean mirrors heaven's grace,
As waves reflect each shining face.
In this vast realm of mysteries,
We sail beneath the cosmic trees.

With guiding stars, our hearts take flight,
To navigate the dreamer's night.
Each cluster whispers secrets bold,
Of journeys past and futures told.

So let us chart our course with care,
In starlit skies, dreams linger there.
For every wave that kisses sand,
Is written in the heavens grand.

Midnight's Comforting Arms

In shadows deep, the midnight breathes,
With tender sighs, the spirit leaves.
Wrapped in silence, peace unfolds,
In twilight's arms, our hearts are bold.

The stars above, a quilt of grace,
In this serene, our fears erase.
With every heartbeat, soft and slow,
Midnight's warmth ignites the glow.

Each whispered word, a calming balm,
A gentle hush, a soothing charm.
In midnight's hold, we drift as one,
Beneath the watchful celestial sun.

So let the world outside drift away,
In this embrace, we long to stay.
For in the dark, there's light within,
In midnight's arms, our souls begin.

Resting Under the Celestial Waves

Moonlight dances on the sea,
Whispers of the stars set free.
Gentle waves cradle my dream,
In this sleep, I'm anchored, it seems.

Softly sighing, night descends,
Nature's lullaby transcends.
Clouds like ships drift in the blue,
In this calm, I start anew.

Dreams of voyages across the tide,
In the embrace of night, I bide.
With each breath, I feel alive,
Under the stars, my heart will thrive.

Here I lay, time drifts away,
Beneath the moon's tender sway.
In the silence, peace I find,
Resting with the stars aligned.

Blissful Harbor of Twilight

As the sun dips, colors bloom,
Painting skies in soft perfume.
Boats rest quiet in the bay,
Listening to the dusk's ballet.

Gentle breezes kiss the shore,
Nature whispers, asking for more.
In this harbor, hearts can mend,
Time and waves seem to suspend.

Stars blink slowly, dreams take flight,
Guiding souls through velvet night.
Each moment here, a treasure kept,
In this blissful harbor, I've wept.

Calm surrounds, like a warm embrace,
Every worry starts to erase.
With twilight's grace, I feel alive,
In this haven, love will thrive.

Sails of Calm on Soft Waters

Sails of white glide after dusk,
Catching wind, a gentle musk.
Ripples whisper tales untold,
Soft waters cradle hearts so bold.

Underneath the vast expanse,
Time unravels in a trance.
No hurry rushes, all is right,
In this silence, dreams ignite.

Horizon stretches, peace unfolds,
In this dance, the world beholds.
Each breath drawn, a moment's grace,
Sails of calm, a soft embrace.

Here I linger, at the seam,
Where the sea and sky redeem.
Buoyant spirits roam the night,
On soft waters, pure delight.

Beneath the Tranquil Horizon

The sun dips low, a fiery glow,
Painting clouds with ember's flow.
Beneath this vast and tranquil line,
Hope and dreams begin to shine.

Golden rays on water glisten,
In this peace, the heart can listen.
Gentle tides pull at the shore,
Whispers of a timeless lore.

Every wave a soft embrace,
Guiding thoughts to a sacred place.
In this calm, we find the core,
Beneath the horizon, we explore.

Stars awaken one by one,
Night unfolds, the day is done.
In this hush, I close my eyes,
Beneath the skies, my spirit flies.

Safe Harbor of Drowsy Beliefs

In twilight's warm embrace we find,
A refuge for the weary mind.
Soft shadows cradle, dreams entwine,
In this haven, calm and kind.

The lapping waves, a gentle song,
Where all our doubts can't linger long.
In whispered winds, the heart grows strong,
Here in this place, we all belong.

Beneath the stars, our thoughts take flight,
In colors of the fading light.
Each secret shared feels oh so right,
In dreams we weave, embracing night.

Together, we shall drift and sway,
In drowsy faith, we'll find our way.
In twilight's glow, we choose to stay,
A safe harbor, come what may.

Whispers of the Tidal Dream

The ocean breathes a soothing sound,
Where tender whispers can be found.
In rhythm with the tides that gleam,
Our souls awaken from their dream.

With every wave that kisses sand,
A promise made, a guiding hand.
The moon reflects on waters deep,
In tranquil nights, our spirits leap.

Seashell secrets softly shared,
Each echo shows how much we cared.
In salty breeze, our hopes take flight,
Bathed in the glow of silver light.

Together we will dance and drift,
In tidal pools, our hearts uplift.
Each moment sways in gentle beams,
In love's embrace, our tidal dreams.

Echoes in the Moonlit Bay

The moon above, a silver guide,
In peaceful waters we confide.
Soft murmurs drift where dreams can play,
In echoes felt, a warm ballet.

Reflections of our whispered care,
In every glance, we find and share.
The night unfolds a tapestry,
In shimmering threads, we're wild and free.

With every turn, the sea breathes low,
The rhythm of the night's soft flow.
In every wave, our laughter swells,
The tale of love, the ocean tells.

Together, here, our hearts align,
With every splash, your hand in mine.
In moonlit grace, we drift away,
Forever caught in this bright bay.

Serenade of the Gentle Waves

The waves compose a soothing song,
In harmony, where we belong.
Their tender lullaby resounds,
In every corner, love surrounds.

With every crest, our spirits soar,
In salty air, we crave for more.
The whispering winds, a soft embrace,
In nature's arms, we find our place.

The sun descends, the colors blend,
A painter's touch, the day shall end.
In twilight's kiss, the waves will dance,
Inviting us to take a chance.

We'll gather dreams, like shells on shore,
In gentle tides that we explore.
A serenade from sea to sky,
In rhythm with our hearts, we'll fly.

A Soothing Whisper to the Horizon

Beneath the painted sky, we stand,
Soft breezes cradle dreams so grand.
Whispers of hope in the twilight glow,
Echoes of love in the evening flow.

The distant waves call out our names,
As stars ignite in gentle flames.
With every sigh, the world feels wide,
A soothing promise, a faithful guide.

Each moment cherished, held so near,
In every heartbeat, there's no fear.
Together we wander, hand in hand,
Towards the horizon, where dreams expand.

The sun dips low, a silent sigh,
Our worries fade as the day bids bye.
In this calm space, we find our way,
A soothing whisper at the end of day.

Gentle Estuary Embrace

Where rivers meet the tender sea,
Nature paints a scene so free.
Gentle currents softly weave,
A tapestry that we believe.

Shimmering sands beneath our feet,
Cradle the rhythm, pure and sweet.
Whispers of life in the cool, moist air,
Invite all souls to pause and stare.

In the twilight's gentle embrace,
The world slows down, finds its place.
Rippling echoes of joy arise,
In this estuary, beneath the skies.

Together we breathe, we feel, we flow,
As time dims softly, our spirits grow.
Nature's hug, a warm retreat,
In this gentle grasp, our hearts beat.

Comfort in the Whispered Waters

Ripples dance upon the lake,
Silent messages they make.
Softly lapping, sweet and slow,
Comfort found in where we go.

Moonlight kisses the tranquil tide,
In its glow, our hearts confide.
A quiet place, where dreams take flight,
With whispered waters anchoring night.

Stars above watch with tender gaze,
In this stillness, our spirits blaze.
Each wave a tale of love and grace,
Carried gently to a sacred place.

In the hush, our worries cease,
Amidst the waters, we find peace.
Together, always, just us two,
In whispered warmth, the world feels new.

Along the Serene Drift

As dawn breaks softly on the shore,
We wander where the waters roar.
Gentle whispers call us near,
In every corner, love appears.

Misty pathways guide our way,
While golden light begins to play.
Nature's canvas, lush and bright,
Awakens all to pure delight.

With every step, our hearts align,
In this serene drift, all is fine.
Lapping waves embrace the sand,
A timeless bond, we understand.

Sunset paints the sky with fire,
In this moment, we aspire.
Together drifting, hearts so free,
Along the waves, just you and me.

Embrace of the Dusk's Tide

The sun dips low, a golden glow,
Whispers of night begin to flow.
Waves caress the sandy shore,
Embracing dusk forevermore.

Stars awake in twilight's hue,
Painting skies in shades of blue.
Gentle breezes start to rise,
As dreams unfurl beneath the skies.

The moon ascends, a silver thread,
Guiding boats as daylight fled.
In the hush, a soft refrain,
Nature sighs, embracing pain.

With every pulse, the tide will sweep,
Carrying whispers into sleep.
In the arms of night we sway,
Lost in dreams till break of day.

Wind Chimes by the Shorelight

Breezes play a sweet refrain,
Wind chimes sing, a soft domain.
Echoes dance on ocean's breath,
Whispers of life, beyond from death.

Salt and song blend in the air,
Joy and peace linger everywhere.
With every note, the waves align,
In harmony, our souls entwine.

Moonlight glimmers on the sea,
Each chime tells a tale, so free.
In this moment, time stands still,
Capturing hearts, the tide fulfills.

As the stars begin to gleam,
We drift softly in a dream.
Wind chimes ringing till the dawn,
A melody forever drawn.

Reverie of the Resting Reef

Beneath the waves, a world so bright,
Colors dance in soft moonlight.
Coral gardens, life abloom,
In the depths, dispelling gloom.

Tides whisper secrets of the deep,
In every corner, shadows creep.
Fish weave tales of ancient lore,
Ebbing currents forevermore.

Gentle currents cradle dreams,
Reflecting sun in shimmering beams.
In the quiet, thoughts take flight,
As the reef bathes in soft light.

A sanctuary, safe and vast,
Memories linger of the past.
In this realm, time drifts away,
Wrapped in nature's pure display.

Celestial Cradle of the Sea

Stars fall down like shimmering tears,
 Cradling dreams, banishing fears.
  Waves embrace the silent night,
   In their arms, a heart takes flight.

  Nebulae twinkle, magic spun,
   Guided by the silvered sun.
    Ocean whispers to the shore,
     Secrets kept, forevermore.

Each crest a journey, fierce and bold,
 Stories of life in blue and gold.
  Here, the universe unfolds,
In the cradle of the waves, we hold.

 As dawn awakens, skies ablaze,
We greet the sun through gentle haze.
  In the ebb and flow, we find,
   The sea's embrace, forever kind.

Dreams Danced at the Water's Edge

Whispers soft upon the sand,
Footprints mark where dreams do stand.
Moonlight weaves through silver tides,
In this world where hope abides.

Fingers trace the ocean's play,
As night sways slowly into day.
Each wave carries a secret thrill,
In the still, the heart is filled.

Stars above in velvet skies,
Mirrored in the sea's deep eyes.
Laughter echoes with the breeze,
As dreams awaken under trees.

Here at the shore, we let love flow,
Where time stands still, and joy will grow.
A dance of dreams, a gentle song,
At the water's edge, we belong.

Echoes of the Swaying Tide

Gentle waves lap on the shore,
Telling tales of days of yore.
Sandcastles built by fleeting light,
Fade away into the night.

The sea calls out, a siren's song,
Where hearts can heal, and dreams belong.
Each cresting rise, each deep blue fall,
Reminds us how we've loved it all.

Seagulls dance with winds so free,
In their flight, we find our glee.
Footprints left, a fleeting trace,
Echoes linger in this place.

The tide moves in, a rhythmic breath,
A soothing pulse, a dance with death.
In the quiet, we hear the call,
Of the ocean's heart, embracing all.

Starlit Beachside Reveries

Under stars that brightly gleam,
We wander lost within a dream.
The waves hum tunes of nights gone by,
As time drifts on, just you and I.

Soft sand cradles each tender sigh,
As moonlight paints the endless sky.
In shadows deep, our stories blend,
Magic whispers, hearts transcend.

Crisp air carries scents divine,
As stars align, our fates combine.
Hand in hand, we walk the line,
Where dreams unfold, and spirits shine.

Each moment shared, a treasure found,
In the silence, love's sweet sound.
Starlit nights, where memories lay,
Beachside reveries, come what may.

Soundtrack of the Restful Bay

Waves murmur low, a soft refrain,
Nature's song beneath the rain.
Whispers dance on ocean sprays,
Creating music for our days.

Swaying trees in tender tune,
Singing softly to the moon.
The bay hums sweet, a lullaby,
As dreams unfold, and spirits fly.

With every tide, old tales revive,
In peaceful rhythms, we arrive.
Quiet moments, hearts entwined,
In this sanctuary, love defined.

Restful bay, a tranquil land,
Where time surrenders, hand in hand.
In nature's grip, we find our way,
To the sweet soundtrack of the bay.

Dreamcatcher of the Expansive Sea

A dreamcatcher sways on the breeze,
Gathering wishes from waves and keys.
Stars twinkle like dreams in the vast,
Whispers of hope from the ocean's past.

It catches the tales of sailors bold,
Of treasures buried and legends told.
With each gentle pull of the tide,
New dreams awaken, anew they glide.

The sea sings softly, a lullaby clear,
Embracing the world in a tender sphere.
Waves crash lightly, a rhythmic dance,
In the heart of the deep, dreams find their chance.

So let your sorrows be swept away,
In the arms of the sea, let your spirit play.
For the dreamcatcher holds, with a loving grace,
The endless wonders of this sacred space.

Moonlit Murmurs of Peace

Beneath the moon's glow, a quiet sigh,
Soft murmurs of night, to the stars we fly.
The world hushes deep, in velvet night,
Finding solace in the silver light.

Each whisper carries a tale untold,
Of dreams wrapped tight in shadows old.
Luna's embrace wraps us in calm,
A gentle warmth, like a sacred psalm.

The winds weave tales through whispering trees,
As peace settles thick on the evening breeze.
In the stillness, hearts start to mend,
As moonlit murmurs, like lovers, blend.

In this serene glow, let worries cease,
Find your heartbeat, feel the release.
For in each moment, lost in the night,
Lies the promise of love, pure and bright.

Tidal Secrets in the Night

Tides uncover secrets upon the shore,
Stories of ages, whispers of yore.
In the night's embrace, they softly wake,
Rising and falling, for memory's sake.

Moonbeams glint on waters deep,
Where shadows and mysteries safely sleep.
Each wave a guardian of dreams and lies,
Guarding the truths where the ocean sighs.

Shells hold stories mute and shy,
From creatures that dance as they drift by.
In the hush of the dark, listen closely now,
For the tide has secrets to share, somehow.

So walk the shoreline, let your spirit soar,
Feel the pulse of secrets from ocean's core.
In the night's quiet grace, find what is true,
Tidal whispers will speak, just for you.

A Symphony of Rest by the Coast

A symphony plays where the waters meet,
With melodies soft, it lulls us sweet.
The waves compose a tranquil song,
Inviting us where hearts belong.

Seagulls cry in harmonious flight,
As the sun dips low, ushering night.
Footsteps trace paths in the golden sand,
In each soft note, we understand.

The ocean hums a cool, soothing tune,
Under the watchful gaze of the moon.
In this concert of stillness, we find our place,
A gentle embrace, a sacred space.

So let go of burdens, embrace the sound,
In this symphony of rest, peace is found.
By the coast, life slows to a serene pace,
As the heart finds its rhythm in this embrace.

Murmurs Beneath the Starry Dome

In the hush of night's embrace,
Whispers dance through space.
Stars flicker with ancient lore,
Echoes of dreams from yore.

The sky, a canvas deep and wide,
Cradles secrets that confide.
Waves of silence gently swell,
Under the moon's silver spell.

Beneath this vast celestial sea,
Hearts connect, wild and free.
Galaxies weave their story,
In starlit paths of glory.

With each breath, the night reveals,
The magic that the darkness feels.
Murmurs travel, soft and bold,
Beneath the dome of dreams untold.

An Ocean's Softest Song

Whispers on the rolling tide,
Secrets that the waves confide.
Each crest a note, each foam a sigh,
An ocean's song beneath the sky.

With every ebb, a tale unfolds,
Of sailors brave and treasures old.
The rhythm sways with gentle grace,
In water's warm, embracing space.

Shells collect the songs of yore,
Carried by the ocean's roar.
A melody soft and true,
Echoes deep in shades of blue.

As twilight brushes skies of gold,
The ocean whispers stories told.
A lullaby to end the day,
In waves that dance and sway.

Tranquil Teal and Silver

In twilight's gentle, muted hue,
Teal meets silver, calm and true.
The water reflects a tender light,
Cradling dreams that take to flight.

Leaves whisper secrets in the breeze,
As shadows tiptoe through the trees.
A tranquil hush envelops all,
Nature's symphony, serene call.

Silvery fish in ripples dart,
Rippling like the beat of a heart.
Each moment savored, held so dear,
In tranquil colors, silence clear.

A canvas painted in soft grace,
Where time slows down and finds its place.
In teal and silver, peace abounds,
Where every whisper softly sounds.

Bebop of the Nighttime Breeze

The night is alive with a lively tune,
Breezes dance 'neath the silver moon.
They tap and swirl with such delight,
   Creating rhythms in the night.

Leaves sway gently, tapping feet,
   The world around finds its beat.
   Stars blink in the cosmic play,
As dreams and whispers float away.

Jazz notes linger in the air,
   Each soft gust a melodic flair.
The moonlight twinkles with a grin,
   Inviting all to join within.

Bebop echoes through the trees,
   A song inspired by the breeze.
   In every twist, a story flows,
Where nighttime magic softly grows.

Tangled in Ocean's Sigh

The waves whisper secrets soft and slow,
Beneath the moon's gentle, silver glow.
Drifting hearts in a salty breeze,
Lost in the dance of the rolling seas.

Stars blink like dreams upon the tide,
Where shadows and light in harmony glide.
Each swell carries stories old and new,
In ocean's sigh, our souls pull through.

Whispers of love in the spray of foam,
We find our way, forever home.
Through ebb and flow, we are bound tight,
In tangled embrace of the tranquil night.

With every crest, we take our flight,
In the ocean's breath, we find our light.
Together we sail, our hearts align,
In the sacred sea, our spirits entwine.

Ripples of Nighttime Tranquility

Softly the night wraps the world so tight,
Moonlit ripples dance in soft flight.
Stars whisper low in tranquil glee,
An echo of dreams floating free.

The water gently cradles the shore,
Each ripple a story, an ancient lore.
Whispers of night weave through tall trees,
Carrying tales on the night's cool breeze.

Calmness settles like dew on grass,
In twilight's glow, moments pass.
A quiet promise in each fading ray,
As silence finds its easing way.

Beneath the sky, hearts beat as one,
In the glow of the setting sun.
Ripples of peace in the nighttime air,
A serenade whispered with gentle care.

Fisherman's Tale of the Night

The nets are cast in shadows deep,
Where moonlight dances, and waters creep.
With every pull, a story unfolds,
Of silvery fish and treasures untold.

Lines cast far, hopes tangled wide,
With patience and care, the sea is our guide.
A whispering breeze through the silent waves,
Each tug on the line, a heart that braves.

Tales of lost nights and catch of the day,
In the quiet of dark, where dreams play.
With lanterns aglow, the shadows merge,
In fisherman's heart, the ocean's urge.

Morning will break with a gentle song,
But for now, in the night, we belong.
Casting our hopes to the deep blue expanse,
In the rhythm of tides, we take our chance.

Twilight's Velvet Embrace

In twilight's glow, the day's sigh fades,
As shadows stretch in soft cascades.
Stars peek out with an eager eye,
In velvet skies where dreams can fly.

The hush of night drapes gently down,
Caressing the world like a silken gown.
A whispered breeze, a soft caress,
In the lingering light, we find our rest.

Colors merge in a painter's hand,
As day gives way to a starlit land.
Moments linger in this sweet embrace,
A cherished pause in the infinite space.

Hold my hand, let the night unfold,
In twilight's arms, we'll be bold.
With every breath, a promise made,
In velvet night, our fears will fade.

Soothe the Stars Above

Under the velvet night sky,
Whispers of dreams gently sigh.
Stars twinkle with a soft light,
Guiding lost souls through the night.

Calm winds carry sweet lullabies,
Cradling thoughts as time flies.
Embrace the peace that they bring,
As the universe starts to sing.

In quiet moments, heart finds rest,
Under the moon's tender jest.
Each twinkle a promise to keep,
Lifting the veil of night's deep.

So close your eyes, let worries cease,
In the arms of the stars, find peace.
With every breath, drift above,
Soothed by the stars we love.

Slumbering Seashell Secrets

On golden sands where shells lie,
Whispers of the ocean sigh.
Cradled by the waves' embrace,
Nature weaves a timeless space.

Each shell tells tales of the deep,
Of secrets that the waters keep.
In moonlight's glow, they softly gleam,
Echoing the sea's sweet dream.

Resting gently, the shore awaits,
While stars align and destiny waits.
In the hush, the currents flow,
Where sea and sky together glow.

Listen closely to their sound,
Magic in each shell is found.
Slumbering secrets softly shared,
In the ocean's arms, we're spared.

Dance of the Twilight Surf

As day bows down to evening's grace,
The waves begin their rhythmic pace.
Twilight paints the sky in hues,
A canvas bright, with evening clues.

Each wave a dancer, wild and free,
Twirling 'neath the whispering sea.
Salt-kissed air, a gentle breeze,
Carries our hearts with such ease.

On shifting sands, we stand in awe,
Of nature's grip, without a flaw.
In each crest and foamy sigh,
The twilight surf bids us goodbye.

Join the dance, let spirits soar,
In this moment, we're evermore.
As the sun dips behind the shore,
The twilight surf sings, forevermore.

Crashing Waves of Night's Rest

The moonlight spills on waters wide,
Crashing waves with a calming tide.
Night wraps the world in velvet hue,
Inviting dreams to drift anew.

With each crash, the shore's embrace,
Calls us to a peaceful place.
In the rhythm of night's sweet song,
We find where we truly belong.

Soft whispers of the ocean's roar,
Guide us gently to the shore.
Let the waves wash worries away,
As night unfolds in sweet ballet.

Cradled in the ocean's chest,
Let the waves of night bring rest.
In the hush, beneath starlit gleam,
We drift into a lingering dream.

Sweet Rest Amongst the Shells

Along the shore where soft winds sigh,
Seashells whisper secrets nigh.
Each grain of sand a tale of old,
Cradled in the sea's gentle fold.

Beneath the sun, a tranquil gleam,
Where time flows like a tender dream.
Resting hearts find peace, serene,
In the warmth of a golden beam.

Tides bring messages from afar,
Singing softly, like a star.
In the cradle of twilight's arms,
Shells vibrate with nature's charms.

Here lies a calm, a soothing hush,
Amongst the waves, a gentle brush.
Sweet rest unfolds in soft hello,
As whispers of the sea bestow.

Lull of the Hidden Depths

In shadows deep where mysteries play,
The ocean's lull will drift away.
Beneath the waves, a silent song,
Where dreams of currents glide along.

Hidden depths of azure blue,
Cradle secrets, old and new.
Gentle whispers call the night,
Guiding stars in soft twilight.

Ripples dance in moonlit glow,
Softly weaving tales below.
Each pulse of water, a breath divine,
A world vibrant, yet entwined.

Sleep now in the ocean's grace,
Where time suspends in its embrace.
Each lullaby, a tide's caress,
Whispers sweet of nature's rest.

Crystalline Echoes of the Night

In the stillness where the shadows play,
Crystalline echoes call the gray.
Moon beams twinkle like a spark,
Illuminating secrets in the dark.

Glistening shores whisper low,
As night unfolds its silent show.
Stars dance upon the rippling sea,
Each reflection holds a memory.

A melody drifts on the breeze,
Where tranquility aims to please.
The night carries tales of old,
In crystalline tones, courage bold.

Rest within this perfect peace,
As the world sighs, anxieties cease.
Let echoes of the night align,
In dreamy rhythms, pure and fine.

Hushed Whispers of a Coastal Dream

On the edge where water meets land,
Hushed whispers curl like grains of sand.
The tide breathes deep, a soft refrain,
A coastal dream in nature's chain.

Seagulls glide with grace so light,
Beneath the cloak of fading light.
Every wave a brush of fate,
Crafts the heart to resonate.

In twilight's arms, the ocean sighs,
Painting colors across the skies.
A tranquil symphony unfolds,
As night enshrouds the world it holds.

Embrace the calm of night's embrace,
With every ripple, find your place.
Breathe in deeply, let dreams unfurl,
In whispered hymns of the gentle swirl.

Milton Keynes UK
Ingram Content Group UK Ltd.
UKHW020635301124
451843UK00006B/120